# READING POWER

# Wayne Gretzky
## Hockey Star
### Heather Feldman

The Rosen Publishing Group's
## PowerKids Press ™
New York

1

For Sophie Megan

Published in 2001 by The Rosen Publishing Group, Inc.
29 East 21st Street, New York, NY 10010

First Edition

Book Design: Michael de Guzman

Photo Credits: p. 5 © ELSA HASCH/ALLSPORT; p. 7 © CP Picture Archive; pp. 9, 11, 15 © ALLSPORT; p. 13 © TODD WARSHAW/ALLSPORT; p. 17 © CORBIS/Mitchell Gerber; p. 19 © IAN TOMLINSON/ALLSPORT; p. 21 © EZRA SHAW/ALLSPORT.

Feldman, Heather.
    Wayne Gretzky: hockey star / Heather Feldman.—1st ed.
        p. cm.— (Reading Power)
    Includes bibliographical references and index.
    ISBN 0-8239-5715-2 (alk. paper)
    1. Gretzky, Wayne, 1961— Juvenile literature. 2. Hockey players— Biography— Juvenile literature. I. Title. II. Series.

GV848.5.G73 F45 2001
796.962'092—dc21
(B)                                                                    00-020589

3 2210 00260 1133

Manufactured in the United States of America

# Contents

Wayne Gretzky is a hockey star.

5

Wayne started playing hockey when he was a young boy.

7

When Wayne was 18 years old, he played for a team called the Oilers. Wayne was number 99 for the Oilers.

The Stanley Cup is the most important prize in hockey. Wayne helped the Oilers win the Stanley Cup.

Wayne played hockey for a lot of teams. He played for the Los Angeles Kings.

Wayne kept a hockey puck from a game. He played against the Oilers in that game. The Oilers were his old team.

Wayne and his wife, Janet, have three children. Wayne loves to spend time with his family.

17

Wayne also played for the New York Rangers. Wayne helped his teammates. He passed them the puck a lot. Wayne always wore number 99.

Wayne does not play hockey anymore. At his last game in 1999, he waved goodbye to his fans. Wayne will always be a hockey hero.

# Glossary

**puck** (PUHK)  The hard, black rubber disk used in the game of ice hockey.

**player** (PLAY-ur)  An athlete in a game.

**Stanley Cup** (STAN-lee KUP)  The prize given to the hockey team that wins the National Hockey League championship.

**team** (TEEM)  A group of players.

Here are more books to read about
Wayne Gretzky and hockey:

*Wayne Gretzky: The Great One*
(Book Report Biographies Series)
Andrew Santella
Franklin Watts, Inc.

*The Magic Hockey Stick*
Peter Maloney and Felicia Zekauskas
Dial Books for Young Readers

To learn more about hockey, check
out this Web site:
http://nhl.com/

# Index

Word Count: 157

## Note to Librarians, Teachers, and Parents

If reading is a challenge, Reading Power is a solution! Reading Power is perfect for readers who want high-interest subject matter at an accessible reading level. These fact-filled, photo-illustrated books are designed for readers who want straightforward vocabulary, engaging topics, and a manageable reading experience. With clear picture/text correspondence, leveled Reading Power books put the reader in charge. Now readers have the power to get the information they want and the skills they need in a user-friendly format.